THE CARE FEEDING OF AN INDEPENDENT BOOKSTORE

THREE INSTRUCTIVE ESSAYS

BY ANN PATCHETT

Ann Patchett

1 | The Bookstore Strikes Back

In late February I am in my basement, which is really a very nice part of my house that is not done justice by the word "basement." For the purposes of this story, let's call it the "Parnassus Fulfillment Center." I have hauled 533 boxed-up hardback copies of my latest novel, *State of Wonder*, from Parnassus, the bookstore I co-own in Nashville, into my car, driven them across town (three trips there, and three trips back), and then lugged them down here to the Parnassus Fulfillment Center. Along with the hardbacks, I have brought in countless paperback copies of my backlist books as well. I sign all these books, and stack them up on one enormous and extremely sturdy table. Then I call for backup: Patrik and Niki from the store, my friend Judy, my mother. Together we form an assembly line, taking the orders off the bookstore's website, addressing mailing labels, writing tiny thank-you notes to tuck inside the signed copies, then bubble-wrapping, taping, and packing them up to mail. We get a rhythm going, we have a system, and it's pretty smooth, except for removing the orders from the website. What I don't understand is that no matter how many orders I delete from the list, the list does not get smaller. We are all work and no progress, and I'm sure something must be going seriously wrong. After all, we've had this website for only a week, and who's to say we know what we're doing? "We know what we're doing," Niki says, and Patrik, who set up the website in the first place, confirms this. They explain to me that the reason the list isn't getting any shorter is that the orders are still coming in.

You may have heard the news that the independent bookstore is dead, that books are dead, that maybe even reading is dead—to which I say, "Pull up a chair, friend. I have a story to tell."

The reason I am signing and wrapping books in my basement is that more orders have come in than the store can handle, and the reason so many orders have come in is that, a few days before, I had been a guest on *The Colbert Report*. After a healthy round of jousting about bookstores versus Amazon, Mr. Colbert held a copy of my novel in front of the cameras and exhorted America to buy it from Amazon—to which I, without a moment's thought (because *without a moment's thought* is how I fly these days) shouted, "No! No! Not Amazon, order it off ParnassusBooks.net and I'll sign it for you." And America took me up on my offer, confirming once and for all that the Colbert Bump is real. That explains how I got stuck in the basement, but fails to answer the larger question: what a writer of literary fiction whose "new" book was already ten months old was doing on *The Colbert Report* in the first place. Hang on, because this is where things start to get weird: I was on the show not because I am a writer, but because I am a famous independent bookseller.

Let's go back to the beginning of the story.

This time last year, the city of Nashville had two bookstores. One was Davis-Kidd, which had been our much-beloved locally owned and operated independent before selling out to the Ohio-based Joseph-Beth Booksellers chain ten years ago. Joseph-Beth moved Davis-Kidd into a mall, provided it with thirty thousand square feet of retail space, and put wind chimes and coffee mugs and scented candles in front of book displays. We continued to call it our "local independent," even though we knew it wasn't really true anymore. Nashville also had a Borders, which was about the same size as Davis-Kidd and sat on the edge of Vanderbilt's campus. (In candor, I should say that Nashville has some truly wonderful used-book stores that range from iconic to overwhelming. But while they play an important role in the cultural fabric of the city, it is a separate role—or maybe that's just the perspective of someone who writes books for a living. We have a Barnes & Noble that is a twenty-minute drive out of town if traffic is light, a Books-a-Million on the western edge of the city near a Costco, and a Target that also sell books. Do those count? Not to me, no, they don't, and they don't count to any other book-buying Nashvillians with whom I am acquainted.)

In December 2010, Davis-Kidd closed. It had been profitable, declared the owners from Ohio who were dismantling the chain, but not profitable enough. Then, in March 2011, our Borders store—also profitable—went the way of all Borders stores. We woke up one morning and found we no longer had a bookstore.

How had this happened? Had digital books led us astray? Had we been lured away by the siren song of Amazon's undercut pricing? Had we been careless, failed to support the very places that had hosted our children's story hours and brought in touring authors and set up summer-reading tables? Our city experienced a great collective gnashing of teeth and rending of garments, but to what extent was Nashville to blame? *Both of the closed stores had been profitable.* Despite the fact that our two bookstores were the size of small department stores and bore enormous rents, they had been making their numbers every month. Nashvillians, I'd like the record to show, had been buying books.

The Nashville Public Library organized community forums for concerned citizens to come together and discuss how we might get a bookstore again. Our library, and I will bless them forever, immediately jumped up to fill the void, hosting readings of orphaned authors whose tours had already been scheduled to include trips to Nashville (including mine), and in every way trying to responsibly tackle the problems we faced as a city in need of a bookstore. Someone went so far as to suggest putting a little bookstore in the library, though selling books in the same building where books were free struck me as a bad plan. Surely, I thought, someone would open a bookstore.

My secret was that I did not much miss those mall-sized Gargantuas. The store I really missed had been gone much longer than they had. Mills was the bookstore of my youth. My sister and I used to walk there every day after school, stopping first to check out the puppies in the pet shop across the street, and then going on to admire the glossy covers of the Kristin Lavransdatter series, which is what girls read after they had finished the Little House on the Prairie books, back before the Twilight books were written. Mills could not have been more than seven hundred square feet small, and the people who worked there remembered who you were and what you read, even if you were ten. If I could have that kind of bookstore, one that valued books and readers above muffins and adorable plastic watering cans, a store that recognized it could not possibly stock every single book that every single person might be looking for, and so stocked the books the staff had read and liked and could recommend, if I could recreate the bookish happiness of my childhood, then maybe I was the person for the job. Or maybe not. I wanted to go into retail about as much as I wanted to go into the army.

"You're like a really good cook who thinks she should open a restaurant," my friend Steve Turner told me over dinner. I had gone to Steve for advice, because he has a particular knack for starting businesses, which has led to his knack for making money. He was trying to talk me down from the ledge. "And anyway, you already have a job."

"I wasn't thinking of working in the bookstore," I said.

He shook his head. "Don't ever think you can start a business and just turn it over to someone else. It never works."

In truth, I left that dinner feeling relieved. I'd been to the oracle and the oracle had told me that mine was a bad idea, which must have been what I'd wanted to hear.

In fact, it was exactly Steve Turner's admonition I was thinking of when I met Karen Hayes the next week. We were introduced by our one friend in common, Mary Grey James. Karen was then a sales rep for Random House, and Mary Grey had been a rep for Harcourt. They had both worked at Ingram, a large book distributor outside of Nashville. Karen, who is tall and pale and very serious in a way that brings pilgrims or homesteaders or other indefatigably hardworking people to mind, meant to open a bookstore. Her plan was to quit her job and devote her life to the project. All she lacked was the money. I suggested, having never considered investing in the book business, and not having been asked to do so, that I could pay for the store and promote it. Karen and I would be co-owners, and Mary Grey would be the store's general manager, thus solving the problem of how I could have a bookstore without having to actually work in a bookstore. We hammered out a tentative plan in the time it took to eat our sandwiches. Then Karen pulled a business plan out of her bag and handed it to me.

"It's called Parnassus Books," she said.

I looked at the word, which struck me as hard to spell and harder to remember. I shook my head. "I don't like it," I said. How many people would know what it meant? (In Greek mythology, Mount Parnassus is the home of literature, learning, and music, and, I think, a few other valuable things.) I had wanted a store called Independent People, after the great Halldor Laxness novel about Iceland and sheep, or perhaps Red Bird Books, as I believed that simple titles, especially those containing colors, were memorable.

"I've always wanted a bookstore called Parnassus," Karen said.

I looked at this woman I didn't know, my potential business partner. I wanted a bookstore in Nashville. Why should I get to name it? "You're the one who's going to work there," I told her.

That night, after talking it over with my husband and then securing a more detailed character reference from Mary Grey, I called Karen. According to her numbers, three hundred thousand dollars would be needed to open a twenty-five hundred square foot bookstore. I told her I was in. This was on April 30th, 2011; in two weeks, I was to leave for the UK leg of the *State of Wonder* book tour. The US leg of the tour started June 7th. Karen was working for Random House until June 10th. "Should I announce this on book tour?" I asked her. I knew I'd be giving interviews all day long during the entire month of June. Should I tell people what we had planned over lunch? That we had a name I didn't like but money in the bank, that we were strangers?

"Sure," Karen said, after some real hesitation. "I guess."

When I look back on all this now I'm dizzied by the blitheness that stood in place of any sort of business sense, the grand gesture of walking over to the roulette table and betting it all on a single number. Anyone I mentioned this plan to was quick to remind me that books were dead, that in two years—I have no idea where "two years" came from, but that figure was consistently thrown at me—books would no longer exist, much less bookstores, and that I might as well be selling eight-track tapes and typewriters. But somehow all the naysaying never lodged itself in my brain. I could see it working as clearly as I could see me standing beside my sister in Mills. I was a writer, after all, and my books sold pretty well. I spoke to crowds of enthusiastic readers all over the country, and those readers were my proof. More than that, I was partnered with Karen Hayes, who wore the steely determination of a woman who could clear a field and plant it herself; and with Mary Grey, my dear friend who had opened a bookstore before. Moreover, our two giant, departed bookstores had been profitable every month; there was the roulette ball bouncing up again and again until finally coming to rest on the number I had chosen.

I would leave soon on my US tour, but Karen and I managed to look at some possible spaces. We were like a couple of newlyweds in an arranged marriage looking for our first apartment. We didn't know what the other one would like, and our conversations were awkward exchanges followed by long periods of awkward silence. One place had only studded two-by-fours for walls, a forlorn toilet lying on its side in the center of the dark room. Karen could see the potential. (Karen, it quickly became clear, has a much greater capacity for seeing potential than I have.) She saw it again in a restaurant space that had been empty for four years. We picked our way carefully towards the kitchen, letting the beams from our flashlights slide over grease-covered refrigerators and stoves. I had eaten in this place as a child, and it was disgusting even then. It was also huge. "Maybe we could partner with someone who wanted to start a cooking school," Karen said, looking at the hulking appliances. We were open to all possibilities. I was certain the men who showed us these spaces had failed to secure bit parts on *The Sopranos* or in *Glengarry Glen Ross*, but were still practicing for the roles. Often I was grateful for the lack of electricity, certain I would see things in those rooms I didn't want to see. I wanted someplace whistle-clean and move-in ready, preferably with built-in cherry shelving. Karen, however, was in the market for cheap. The place we both favored had once been a sushi restaurant and now had a lien against it. When the manager finally got around to giving us an answer, it was a pronouncement that bookstores were dead and that he wouldn't rent to us at any price.

And so, without a location or anything like an opening date, I left for my book tour, and on the first day announced on the *Diane Rehm Show* that, along with my partner, Karen Hayes, I would be opening an independent bookstore in Nashville. I was vague on every detail, but when asked about the name, I managed to say "Parnassus."

Early in the tour I got a phone call from The Beveled Edge, the frame shop in Nashville where I had long done business. They asked if I wanted them to sell my new book. My alterations shop, Stitch-It, followed suit. I was extremely grateful to be able to tell people in my hometown where they could go to find my novel, but the experience made me feel the loss of a real bookstore more acutely. Parnassus was a good idea for Nashville, yes, but selling books was also in my own best interest.

State of Wonder was my sixth novel and eighth book, and while I've been on many book tours, this one brought with it an entirely new sense of purpose. I was going out to bookstores to read and sign, sure, but I was also there to learn. I wanted to know how many square feet each store had, and how many part-time employees, and where they got those good-looking greeting cards. Booksellers do not guard their best secrets: they are a generous tribe, and were quick to welcome me into their fold and to give me advice. I was told to hang merchandise from the ceiling whenever possible, because people long to buy whatever requires a ladder to cut it down. The children's section should always be in the back corner of the store, so that when parents inevitably wandered off and started reading, their offspring could be caught before they busted out of the store. I received advice about bookkeeping, bonuses, staff recommendations, and websites.

While I was flying from city to city, Karen was driving around the South in a U-haul buying up shelving at rock-bottom prices from various Borders stores that were liquidating. I had written one check before I left, for a hundred and fifty thousand dollars, and I kept asking if she needed more money. No, she didn't need more money.

At the end of the summer, Karen and I finally settled on a former tanning salon a few doors down from a doughnut shop and a nail emporium. Unlike the property managers we had encountered earlier in our quest, the one responsible for this location was a business-savvy Buddhist who felt a bookstore would lend class to his L-shaped strip mall, and to this end was willing to foot the bill to have the tile floors chipped out. The space was long and deep, with ceilings that were too high for us to ever dream of hanging things from. The tanning beds were carted away, but the sign over the door stayed up for a ridiculously long time: TAN 2000. I went to Australia on yet another leg of my book tour, leaving all the work on Karen's head.

The word had spread to the Southern Hemisphere. In Australia, all anyone wanted to talk about was the bookstore. Journalists were calling from Germany and India, wanting to talk about the bookstore. Every interview started off the same way: Hadn't I heard the news? Had no one thought to tell me? Bookstores were over. Then, one by one, the interviewers recounted the details of their own favorite stores, and I listened. They told me, confidentially and off the record, that they thought I just might succeed.

I was starting to understand the role the interviews would play in that success. In my thirties, I had paid my rent by writing for fashion magazines. I found *Elle* to be the most baffling because its editors insisted on identifying trends. Since most fashion magazines "closed" (industry jargon for the point at which the pages are shipped to the printing plant) three months before they hit the newsstands, the identification of trends, especially from Nashville, required an act of near-clairvoyance. Eventually, I realized what everyone in fashion already knew: a trend is whatever you call a trend. *This spring in Paris, fashionistas will wear fishbowls on their heads.* In my hotel room in Australia, this insight came back to me more as a vision than as a memory. "The small independent bookstore is coming back," I told reporters in Berlin and Bangladesh. "It's part of a trend."

My act was on the road, and with every performance I tweaked the script, hammering out the details as I proclaimed them to strangers: All things happen in a cycle, I explained—the little bookstore had succeeded and grown into a bigger bookstore. Seeing the potential for profit, the superstore chains rose up and crushed the independents, then Amazon rose up and crushed the superstore chains. Now that we could order any book at any hour without having to leave the screen in front of us, we realized what we had lost: the community center, the human interaction, the recommendation of a smart reader rather than a computer algorithm telling us what other shoppers had purchased. I promised whomever was listening that from those very ashes the small independent bookstore would rise again.

What about the e-books, the journalists wanted to know. How can you survive the e-books?

And so I told them—I care *that* you read, not *how* you read. Most independent bookstores, and certainly Barnes & Noble, are capable of selling e-books through their websites, and those e-books can be downloaded onto any e-reader except for Amazon's Kindle, which worked only for Amazon purchases. So you can support a bookstore in your community and still read a book on your iPad.

Say it enough times and it will be true.

Build it and they will come.

In Melbourne, I gave a reading with Jonathan Franzen. I asked him if he would come to the bookstore. Sure, he said, he'd like to do that. Down in the Antipodes, my mind began to flip through my Rolodex. I know a lot writers.

Meanwhile, back in Nashville, Karen and Mary Grey had hired a staff, and together they washed the warehoused Borders bookshelves again and again while they waited for the paint to dry and the new flooring to arrive. In a burst of optimism, we had hoped to open October 1st. Lights were still missing when we finally did open on November 15th. We had forgotten to get cash for the cash register, and I ran to the bank with my checkbook. That morning, the *New York Times* ran a story about the opening of Parnassus, along with a photo of me, on page A1.

Imagine a group of highly paid consultants crowded into the offices of my publisher, Harper Collins. Their job is to try and figure out how to get a picture of a literary novelist (me, say) on the front page of the *Times*. "She could kill someone," one consultant suggests. The other consultants shake their heads. "It would have to be someone very famous," another says. "Could she hijack a busload of school children, or maybe restructure the New York public school system?" They sigh. It would not be enough. They run down a list of crimes, stunts, and heroically good deeds, but none of them are Page One material. I can promise you this: kept in that room for all eternity, they would not have landed on the idea that opening a twenty-five hundred square foot bookstore in Nashville would do the trick.

The bookstore that does in fact open in Nashville is so beautiful I can't even make sense of it. While I've spent the summer talking, Karen has taken her dreams out of the air. She has made the ideal bookstore of her own imagination into a place where you can actually come and buy books. I realize now my business partner is something of a novelist herself. She attended to the most tedious details, and then went on to make a work of art. Through every color choice, every cabinet, every twinkling hanging star, she had conjured a world that was worth inexpressibly more than the sum of its dazzling parts, the kind of bookstore children will remember when they are old themselves. Parnassus, I could finally see, was perfectly named, as she had known all along it would be. Every time I walk through the door I think, Karen was the one person I met who wanted to open a bookstore, and how did I have the sense upon meeting her to sign on for life?

On opening day, National Public Radio wanted an interview from the store. They wanted background noise, but too many people made too much background noise and we had to retreat to the back corner of the storage room. The *CBS Morning Show* called at four o'clock that afternoon. I would have to get on a plane in the next two hours to be on CBS in the morning. When we had our grand opening the following Saturday, an all-day extravaganza that stretched from early-morning puppet shows to late-night wine and cheese, an estimated three thousand Nashvillians came through the store, devouring books like locusts sweeping through a field of summer wheat. All of us who worked there (not a number I normally include myself in, but in this case I was among them) had waited so long for customers that once they finally came we could not stop telling them what we wanted them to read. One more joy I had failed to consider: that I can talk strangers into reading books that I love. The shelves we had so recently washed and dried and loaded down were startlingly empty. Karen kept running back to the office to order yet more books, while I kept climbing onto a bench to make yet another speech. Every local television news program came, every local newspaper, along with *People* magazine. I was interviewed so many times a person walking past the window of our bookstore on his way to the Donut Den might think that we had won the Derby, or cured cancer, or found a portal to the South Pole.

"You know," I had told Karen early on, "you're going to wind up doing all the work and I'm going to get all the credit. That could get really annoying."

But she didn't seem annoyed, either by the abstract concept or, later, by the omnipresent and unavoidable reality. "You just do your job," she told me. "I'll do mine."

My job has become something I could never have imagined, and while it surely benefits Parnassus, Parnassus is not exactly the point. Without ever knowing that such a position existed, let alone that it might be available, I have inadvertently become the spokesperson for independent bookstores. People still want books; I've got the numbers to prove it. I imagine they remember the bookstores of their own youth with the same tenderness that I remember mine. They are lined up outside most mornings when we open our doors because, I think, they have learned through this journey we've all been on that the lowest price is not always the best value. Parnassus Books creates jobs in our community and contributes to the tax base. We've made a place to bring children to learn and to play, and to think those two things are one and the same. We have a piano. We have a dachshund. We have authors who come and read, and you can ask them questions, and they will sign your book. The business model may be antiquated, but it's the one that I like, and so far it's the one that's working.

And maybe it's working because I'm an author, and maybe it's working because Karen works like an entire horseful of Trojans, or because we have a particularly brilliant staff, or because Nashville is a city that is particularly sympathetic with all things independent. Maybe we just got lucky. But the way this luck feels is that changing the course of the corporate world is possible. Amazon doesn't get to make all the decisions; the people can make them by how and where they spend their money. If what a bookstore offers matters to you, then shop at a bookstore. If you feel that the experience of reading a book is valuable, then read the book. This is how we change the world: We grab hold of it. We change ourselves.

(*The Atlantic Monthly*, November 2012)

2 | Things No One Told Me About Owning a Bookstore

Not too long ago I went to Whole Foods at 8:30 at night. It's not my normal grocery hour but it had been a busy day. Evenings are when the hipsters venture out, the twenty-somethings and the single men. As I steered my cart between the chocolate and the cheese, I was stopped by an impossibly chic couple. Songwriters? Movie stars? They asked me if I was the bookstore lady, and when I told them yes, I was, they leaned in to confide. Their daughter did not like to read. They had read to her from birth! They had held her in their laps and turned the pages and made the whole thing fun and warm but the daughter was impervious to their good example. Now she was eight and she had no interest in books. They were panicked. They were not entirely sure how she could be their child.

"I have two words for you," I said. "Captain Underpants."

They blinked. They knew nothing of *Captain Underpants.* They had been shooting for *The Secret Garden, The Little Princess,* beautiful books that would not solve the problem. But even in the cheese aisle I knew this child needed Dav Pilkey's subversive elementary-school readers. Books for children who felt uncomfortable with reading.

"Go to the back of the bookstore and tell them you need a dog. They're usually asleep under the desks. Get a dog and a copy of *Captain Underpants*. Let your daughter read the book to the dog." I told them that Opie, a large hound mix owned by our store manager, was a particularly reliable candidate.

The beautiful hipsters shook my hand reverentially and we said goodnight, pushing our carts in different directions. I was reminded yet again that there is nothing better than owning a bookstore.

When I first met Karen Hayes in 2011 and we decided to go into business together, I viewed opening an independent bookstore as a civic obligation, an unwanted but necessary ordeal. We were without a bookstore in Nashville and, well, somebody had to do it. I thought of the Sisters of Mercy who had overseen my education from first grade through high school. Their consistent message was one of duty: If you see the trash, the trash is yours to pick up. If you have the time to formulate in your head the sentence *I wonder whose responsibility it is to*_____ (fill in the blank: *solve global warming, feed the poor, overhaul the public education system*), you can bet that the responsibility is yours. Once I realized this bookstore situation wasn't going to solve itself, I gave a heavy sigh and trudged ahead. I had no idea that the door I was about to open would be the one that would flood my world with light.

The doomsayers took no small amount of pleasure in cautioning Karen and me that bookstores were dead, that books were dead, that we were fools in a small canoe paddling straight towards Niagara Falls. Everyone had a list of potential risks they were anxious to share with us, and yet not one person mentioned the potential rewards. I am here to report: We did not plunge over the falls, and the rewards have been incalculable. In hopes of encouraging anyone who dreams of opening an independent bookstore, and with thanks to everyone who shops in one, I hereby set down a partial list of the unanticipated dividends.

EMPLOYEES

Would you like a group of friends you could get together with any time? Smart, funny friends with wide-ranging personalities who have interests similar to your own? Owning a bookstore is the closest I'm ever going to come to living in a well-written sitcom. The employees of Parnassus Books are the cast of the old *Dick Van Dyke Show*. We are Mary Tyler Moore's newsroom, the coffee shop of *Friends*, the *Cheers* bar. We employ twelve people full time and five people part time. We make each other birthday cakes, dog-sit for each other's dogs, borrow each other's clothes, mourn each other's losses, dance at each other's weddings, deliver meals when one of us is sick, exchange YouTube videos of sloths, and talk about books. Mostly we talk about books. The people we've hired are so extraordinary that I've often wondered what they're doing working in a bookstore. Why aren't they off running Google? For most of them it's because there wouldn't be enough time in the day to both work and to read, and at least at the bookstore they can read while they're working. Stephanie measures her vacations not by where she went or what she saw, but by how many books she read while she was gone. When she comes back, she piles up the stack of books she's completed by her desk just in case we'd like to discuss any of them.

Andy once said it was the only place he'd ever worked where, if everyone went in together and bought a lottery ticket that won, no one would quit their job.

This is not to say there haven't been some mistakes along the way. We once had an employee who found a dead mouse in the parking lot and laid it gently on a napkin and put it in the freezer in the break room. We discovered the mouse and objected strongly to its presence in our freezer, but our employee said she wasn't about to waste it. Frozen mice, she told us, were fabulous for pranks.

DOGS

At some point in history, dogs had jobs. They herded sheep and ran alongside firetrucks. Rin Tin Tin and Lassie built dazzling careers out of showing how indispensable they could be. But most modern dogs are free of responsibilities. They have nothing to do, and so they curl up for another nap. Lexington changed all of that.

Lexington was a sweet-natured black and tan miniature dachshund who came to work with Niki, our events manager. I don't remember there being any permission requested or granted about bringing a dog to the store. If Niki was there, Lexington was there, and we liked it that way. That dog could sell a book just by sitting on it. Not long after we opened, I adopted Sparky, a little terrier-ish mix, from the shelter and he learned how to fit in fast. Shop dogs must be patient when squeezed by children. They must be willing to be chased. They should be able to roll over and sit up and shake hands. Lexington could also fall over at the command *Bang! Bang!* But then Lexington was a genius.

Two small shop dogs worked out well, but neither was a full-time employee. The standard for full-time dogs was set by the aforementioned Opie, a large hound mix who was adopted by our store manager, Andy. Opie was patient and solid, a real adult. No one could object to Opie.

Which led to Bear. Sissy, our night manager, had neighbors who moved away and left her their dog. Bear might have been wolflike in his youth but his youth had long since passed. Now he was threadbare, snaggle-toothed, and given to peeing on everything. Once Sissy figured out that he could wear a belt lined with a giant Kotex (what we discreetly refer to as his "tinkle belt"), the problem of his continued employment was solved. When he is asleep in his dog bed beneath the table in the children's section there is usually a child in the bed curled up next to him.

So Catherine started bringing her dog Belle, which was understandable, of course; other people get to bring their dogs so why shouldn't she get to bring hers? But Belle, who is a cross between a yellow Lab and an angora rabbit, is very shy and stays in the storeroom under a table. When one of us crawls under the table to visit her she is very happy.

Then Lexington died. This is too sad to speak about. She has a memorial bench in the store where people can sit and think of her. After a long period of mourning, Niki got a dappled dachshund puppy named Mary Todd Lincoln. She has her own Instagram account. People come to Parnassus just to see Mary Todd Lincoln.

In much the same way that not every employee is a good fit, not every dog is shop-dog material. Mary Laura brought her tiny beagle Eleanor Roosevelt into work once, but then some fool opened the door. Tristan, who orders books and is the store's fastest runner, chased her across five lanes of raging afternoon traffic and through a parking garage before catching her just as she was about to enter Nordstrom. Now Eleanor Roosevelt works from home while Mary Laura chronicles the adventures of all the dogs in "The Shop Dog Diaries" for our online literary magazine, *Musing*.

At one point we considered having a café in the store until it occurred to us the health department would make us fire all the dogs. We decided our customers could find another place to have coffee.

CUSTOMERS

All my life I've been telling people what to read. Ask my family, ask my friends. It's the habit of all passionate readers. When you read a book you love, the experience is not complete until you can turn around and say to someone else, "You have to read this book. *You will love this book.*" Every day we throw open the doors of the bookstore and wait for our customers to come in so that we can tell them all about books we love. They want to know which book they should buy for their mother, their teacher, their husband at home with the flu. They want just the right book to take to the host of a dinner party. They want a book that will make them laugh the way they laughed when they read *Where'd You Go, Bernadette,* and cry the way they cried when they read *A Lesson Before Dying.* And we have the answers! No one told me this when I said I was going to open a bookstore. No one told me how good it would feel to put books into the hands of strangers and see their faces light up with a sense of connection. I feel like a revival preacher who has finally pitched her own tent: *Come gather 'round and I'll tell you what to read.*

I love our customers as much as I love the books, and I love the thought of our customers and the books being happy together. I love our customers for keeping our bookstore open, because they do, every time they choose to walk into Parnassus instead of buying their books online. There is the very real sense that every independent bookstore belongs to its customers and to their con-viction that picking up physical books—hefting them, breathing in their new-book scent, considering the typeface—is a worthwhile endeavor. A thousand blessings on the heads of our customers who believe that it's helpful to talk about books with smart Grace at the cash register, not only to get recommendations but to offer them in kind. Our customers browse, slipping into a big leather chair when they find something that merits further consideration. Our customers fold their children into their laps and read them a book. They can count on the fact that one of the dogs will wander over and say hello. With every book our customers buy, they cast a vote for Story Time, for author readings, for the book club Kathy runs at the store that has become so popular she now hosts three sessions of it every month. Book by book, our customers vote against free overnight shipping in favor of a community of book lovers. They vote for *us*, and I could not love them more.

Parnassus Books, which is located in an unlovely strip mall between a Sherwin-Williams paint store and Fleet Feet running shoes, in an area of town jammed up with traffic, has become a vacation destination for readers from across the country. People take trips to Nashville to visit our store. Families come, entire book clubs come, and want their pictures taken with the dogs and sometimes with me. These customers have driven from Minnesota and flown from California. They ask me with unfailing politeness if it wouldn't be too much trouble, if it wasn't asking too much, would I please sign a book for them? I want to clap my hands on their shoulders, put my face right in their face, and say, "Are you *kidding* me? You are the customer. I *love* you."

AUTHORS

If you want to see hummingbirds, plant a bank of salvia in your backyard. If you want to see authors, build a bookstore. My friends—Elizabeth McCracken, Donna Tartt, Jane Hamilton, Maile Meloy, Elizabeth Gilbert, Kevin Wilson—finish their books and go on tour; they eat their oatmeal in my kitchen now. Why hadn't I thought of this earlier? If I wanted to see more of my far-flung writer friends, all I needed to do was give them a perch on which to land. I gave Ruth Reichl my bottle of vitamin C to ward off her book-tour cold. Sparky made off with half of Barbara Kingsolver's grilled cheese sandwich. I tested the bed in my guest room the day before Edwidge Danticat was due to arrive and decided the mattress was as hard as a rock, so I went out and bought a new one. I had loved Edwidge's books for so long, the least I could do was make sure she had a good night's sleep.

Not that we have to go so far afield to find great writers. It turns out Nashville is loaded with them: Andrew Maraniss, Ruta Sepetys, Alice Randall, Adam Ross–I could go on all day! Our local author table is the most popular spot in the store.

Before we opened a bookstore, I had wondered if going to so many author readings would turn out to be something of a drag. To the contrary: they thrill me. The truth is, if you're always on book tour the only show you see is your own. I love to watch how other people work: Margaret Atwood is so much smarter than the rest of us mere mortals I could listen to her all night. Louise Erdrich and Isabel Allende were the most compassionate authors, taking every question from the audience straight into their hearts. Joshua Ferris, Jon Meacham, and T. C. Boyle pulled off very different versions of literary stand-up comedy. All three amazed me. Patti Smith was sick as a dog but, trouper that she is, she found a pocket of strength inside herself and went on to give a thrilling performance. Pat Conroy was the kindest man, shaking the hand of every person in line and introducing himself as Pat Conroy. The hands-down favorite of our staff and, I would imagine, the hands-down favorite of everyone who has ever met her, is Doris Kearns Goodwin. If you ever get the chance to see Doris, move heaven and earth to do so.

And children's book authors? I had never known them before and it turns out they're the nicest people on earth. I had always believed that firefighters topped the list for professional kindness and decency, but now I want to place children's authors right up there next to them. Among them: Jon Klassen, of *I Want My Hat Back* fame; Tad Hills, who writes the *Rocket* and *Duck & Goose* books; Mo Willems, who created the Elephant and Piggie series, not to mention all those pigeon capers; Sandra Boynton (who signed a copy of *Snuggle Puppy* for Sparky); Dav Pilkey, of course, *Captain Underpants* himself (who bought gift certificates from the store to give as gifts to the children in his audience, and then sent a giant box of chocolates to the staff); and Jeff Kinney, *The Wimpy Kid*, who has recently opened a glorious bookstore in his hometown. It's one thing to meet nice people, but when you get to see them being very nice to adoring children, well, that's another matter entirely.

If you are inclined to envy me at all, then envy me for this: I can't believe how lucky I am to get to meet these people and to sit and listen to what they have to say.

BOOKS

My friend Elizabeth McCracken is the most indiscriminate reader I have ever known. She began her professional life as a shelver at her public library when she was in high school. She told me she would read alphabetically, so that in shelving "A" she read Lloyd Alexander to Louis Auchincloss to Jane Austen to V. C. Andrews to Sherwood Anderson to Jean Auel (actual examples). When shelving "C" she read a novel by Winston Churchill.

I get that now. The reading life I once cherished has been tossed into a blender. In the past two weeks I've read *It's Your World*, Chelsea Clinton's book on motivating children to social activism; *Lab Girl*, a wonderful debut memoir by Hope Jahren on becoming a scientist; and Margaret Atwood's classic 2000 novel *The Blind Assassin* (because while my reading has become considerably more eclectic and more current than my pre-bookselling days of poring over Henry James, I do not wish to be entirely of the moment). I read everything now. I am forever falling in love with books that won't be out for months. I was in love with Paul Kalanithi's memoir *When Breath Becomes Air* before anyone else had a copy. I longed for the day I could stand at the cash register and press it in the hands of every customer. I sing the praises of Elizabeth Strout's *My Name is Lucy Barton*, Katy Simpson Smith's gorgeous *Free Men*, Edna O'Brien's terrifying *The Little Red Chairs*, and Jane Hamilton's truly excellent *The Excellent Lombards*—none of which is yet available as I'm writing this.

Being in the presence of so many books, I read what my fellow booksellers recommend (Andy put me on to William Finnegan's *Barbarian Days: A Surfing Life*, a book I loved and never would have picked up on my own), or what catches my eye on our New Releases table (Gloria Steinem's *My Life on the Road*, because who could just walk past that picture of Gloria Steinem and not pick it up?). I buy books of photography (Melissa Ann Pinney's perfect *Two*), books of poetry (James Tate's beautiful final collection, *Dome of the Hidden Pavilion*, that Nathan, the store's poetry expert, put front and center). There are so many things I would have missed were I not in the presence of actual physical books, which is often the reason our customers come in. Instead of knowing what they're going to read next, they come in to see what book demands their attention.

Of course any book someone hasn't read before is a new book to them, which is another great thing about owning a bookstore. I can sell *Act One* by Moss Hart with the same fervor with which someone else might be pushing the new Robert Galbraith thriller.

I can press a copy of Lampedusa's *The Leopard* into the hands of someone who's never heard of it before. (I can get choked up when I think about the pleasure of reading *The Leopard* for the first time.) I can sell Carol Shields's books as if they were just hot off the press. I can introduce a stranger to *The All of It* by Jeannette Haien. I can go on with this joy forever because our customers will never have read all the old books, no one will, and the new books come in as regularly as waves hit a beach.

People have asked me if owning a bookstore has taken time away from my writing, and the answer is yes, it has, but then so has having a dog, and a husband, and a mother who lives down the street, and so many wonderful friends. And like the dog and the husband and the mother and the friends, all of whom I love very much, the benefits the bookstore brings have far outweighed the costs. So if you think you have what it takes to open a bookstore, I urge you to join us. We're having a wonderful time. And if you don't feel the need to own a bookstore, and think that it's enough to just be a part of one, I want to thank you and welcome you on behalf of independent booksellers everywhere. You make us possible, and we're so glad you're here. We've got a book you're going to love.

3 | **Booksellers Love To Recommend Books**
(It's Who We Are)

52 ALL-TIME FAVORITE BOOKS FROM THE YEAR I TURNED 52

1) **Humboldt's Gift**
   by Saul Bellow
   More reader-friendly than *Herzog* or *The Adventures of Augie March*, while still containing the full force of Bellow's brilliance.

2) **Dandelion Wine**
   by Ray Bradbury
   My mother gave me this book for my 13th birthday and I carried it with me everywhere so I could read it over and over again.

3) **In Cold Blood**
   by Truman Capote
   Capote invented a new kind of narrative nonfiction with this book and in doing so made the Clutter family, their murderers, and himself immortal.

4) **The Long Goodbye**
   by Raymond Chandler
   "When in doubt, have a man come through the door with a gun in his hand." – Raymond Chandler. It works.

5) **Selected Stories of Anton Chekhov**

There are so many stories, so many different collections and translations. What matters is that you read them. I favor Richard Pevear's and Larissa Volokhonsky's translation.

6) **The Stories of John Cheever**

"Goodbye, My Brother" is one of the most perfect stories ever written, and once you read that one you won't want to stop.

7) **Jonathan Strange & Mr. Norrell**

by Susanna Clarke
The story of the revival of English magic is 782 pages. I wanted it to be twice that long, and so I read it twice.

8) **Brother, I'm Dying**

by Edwidge Danticat
This is everything a memoir should be: the personal becomes universal by way of compassionate telling.

9) **The Long Loneliness**

by Dorothy Day
The book I go back to when I wonder what it might be like to be a better person.

10) **David Copperfield**

by Charles Dickens
The best orphan in the history of literature. Aunt Betsey, the best aunt in the history of the world.

11) **We Tell Ourselves Stories in Order to Live, Collected Nonfiction**

by Joan Didion
These essays create an essential portrait of 20th century America. They will also tell you everything you need to know about writing nonfiction.

12) **What Is the What?**

by Dave Eggers
This is Eggers' true heartbreaking work of staggering genius. The tale of one of the Lost Boys of the Sudan.

13) **The Great Gatsby**

by F. Scott Fitzgerald
It doesn't matter if you read it in high school. Read it again. It's a perfect novel.

14) **The Blue Flower**

by Penelope Fitzgerald
A young man falls in love with a dying child who is inexplicably mesmerizing. The crazy part is I fell in love with her, too.

15) **Madame Bovary**
by Gustave Flaubert
Flaubert was put on trial for the
corrupting power of this novel
about a woman who is corrupted
by reading novels.

16) **Everything Is Illuminated**
by Jonathan Safran Foer
The only book that has ever
made me both laugh out loud
and sob unexpectedly. A tour de
force.

17) **The Good Solider**
by Ford Maddox Ford
"This is the saddest story I have
ever heard." Which happens to be
my favorite opening line.

18) **The Lost Estate (Le Grand
Meaulnes)**
by Alain-Fournier
A boy gets lost and stumbles
into a world of beauty beyond
imagination. I dream about this
book.

19) **Living; Loving; Party Going**
by Henry Green
"Green's novels reproduce as
few do the actual sensation of
living." --Elizabeth Bowen
Living is my favorite.

20) **The End of the Affair**
by Graham Greene
A passionate love affair is
upended by an inconvenient
love of God. Greene does more
with Catholicism than any other
writer.

21) **The All of It**
by Jeanette Haien
A husband, a wife, a priest, a
deathbed confession, a tale of
Ireland. Once you start there's no
putting it down.

22) **Act One: An Autobiography**
by Moss Hart
Half a life story from a man
so elegant, brilliant, funny, and
determined, you'll fall in love
with him, forgetting that he's
dead.

23) **The Ambassadors**
by Henry James
In a different James novel, it is
said that Isabel Archer isn't just
loved, she is adored, which sums
up my feelings for Henry James
books, this one in particular.

24) **The Unbearable Lightness of Being**
by Milan Kundera
When I first read this book in 1985, I thought it was the most important political/sexual/transcendental novel ever written. I still do.

25) **The Leopard**
by Giuseppe di Lampedusa
The book that makes me anticipate my own death with joy. Top that.

26) **Independent People**
by Halldór Laxness
Sheep. Isolation. Black coffee. Very possibly my favorite novel.

27) **A Perfect Spy**
by John le Carré
This book has a very confusing start, but if you stick with it the payoff is astonishing. Le Carré's greatest novel, according to le Carré.

28) **The Magic Mountain**
by Thomas Mann
The book that most influenced my writing: A group of strangers are thrown together by circumstance.

29) **One Hundred Years of Solitude**
by Gabriel Garcia Márquez
A book that gives the reader an entire world. I will always think about the little gold fish Colonel Aureliano Buendía made.

30) **So Long, See You Tomorrow**
by William Maxwell
Maxwell's mother died in the great flu epidemic of 1918 when he was ten years old. Everything he wrote went back to that. This is his very best.

31) **The Pursuit of Love / Love in a Cold Climate**
by Nancy Mitford
The only problem with these books is that there will never be anything as satisfying again. Ever.

32) **Selected Stories / Family Furnishings**
by Alice Munro
The first volume takes us up to 1994. The second volume goes through 2014. Is this cheating? No, it's just more Alice Munro stories.

33) **Lolita**
by Vladimir Nabokov
Humbert Humbert is in love
with his stepdaughter. Nabokov is
in love with the English language.
I am in love with this book.

34) **The Collected Stories**
by Grace Paley
Grace was my teacher in college
and my role model in life. Her
stories are alive with her voice.

35) **Binocular Vision**
by Edith Pearlman
No doubt the most brilliant and
unsung short story writer of our
age. This book is her masterpiece.

36) **The Human Stain**
by Philip Roth
How Roth never won the Nobel
will remain for me literature's
greatest mystery. This one is my
favorite.

37) **Nine Stories**
by J.D. Salinger
The Catcher in the Rye is a book
for the young. *Nine Stories* is a
book for your entire life.

38) **The Emigrants**
by W. G. Sebald
I read all of Sebald's novels in
a mesmerized binge. I don't
remember loving one more than
the others. I suggest you read
them all.

39) **Her First American**
by Lore Segal
This is a flawed book about
flawed people who have been
completely real to me since the
first time I read it (and I've read it
many times).

40) **The Stone Diaries**
by Carol Shields
Birth to death novels are nearly
impossible to write. This one
is perfect. I prefer the edition
without the photographs.

41) **Endless Love**
by Scott Spencer
Wildly obsessive, disquieting, sexy.
The narrator achieves a level of
emotional insight I have not.

42) **The Patrick Melrose Novels**
by Edward St. Aubyn
These are crazy, drug-doused
fever dream books that I was
addicted to. Be sure you get
the final volume, *At Last*. It's
published separately.

43) **The Little Friend**
by Donna Tartt
My favorite Tartt novel. It captures Mississippi like no other book. That's saying something.

44) **Anna Karenina**
by Leo Tolstoy
Richard Pevear and Larissa Volokhonsky, translators.
I read it at 21 and only cared about Anna and Vronsky. I read it at 50 and cared only about Kitty and Levin.

45) **The Story of Lucy Gault**
by William Trevor
A tiny novel about a tremendous misunderstanding. It's my favorite Trevor, but any Trevor will do.

46) **The Rabbit Angstrom Novels**
by John Updike
No need to go to graduate school in creative writing. Just stay home and read these four books. It was the best home schooling I ever received.

47) **A Handful of Dust**
by Evelyn Waugh
Because there is so much to laugh about in this novel, the tragedy seems almost unbearable. Read *Brideshead Revisited* when you're done.

48) **The Collected Stories of Eudora Welty**
Like Emily Dickinson, Eudora Welty proves that observation, imagination, and compassion are the soul of writing.

49) **Miss Lonelyhearts**
by Nathanael West
These letters to an advice columnist contain all the suffering of the world. The book is best purchased with *Day of the Locust*.

50) **Charlotte's Web**
by E. B. White
This is where literature started for me: a girl, a pig, a spider. The book made me both a writer and a vegetarian.

51) **The Duke of Deception**
by Geoffrey Wolff
This book is often overlooked in favor of his brother Tobias' childhood memoir *This Boy's Life*. But this one is the real genius.

52) **The Complete Poems of W.B. Yeats**
I'll take this with me to the desert island where I'll have time to commit them all to memory.

Ann Patchett is the author of six novels, *The Patron Saint of Liars, Taft, The Magician's Assistant, Bel Canto, Run*, and *State of Wonder*. She was the editor of *Best American Short Stories* in 2006, and has written three books of nonfiction: *Truth & Beauty*, about her friendship with the writer, Lucy Grealy, *What Now?* an expansion of her graduation address at Sarah Lawrence College; and, most recently, *This is the Story of a Happy Marriage*, a collection of essays that examines the theme of commitment. She is co-owner of Parnassus Books in Nashville, TN.

www.parnassusbooks.net